Ebook Entrepreneur:

Crafting Your Path To Profits

By: Richard D. Krause

While every precaution has been taken in the preparation of this book, the publisher assumes no responsibility for errors or omissions, or for damages resulting from the use of the information contained herein.

EBOOK ENTREPRENEUR: CRAFTING YOUR PATH TO PROFIT

First edition. October 2, 2023.

ISBN: 979-8223861188

Written by Richard Krause.

Also by Richard Krause

The Elderly Trap: Uncovering Scams and Reclaiming Security in the Golden Years.
The Spice Cabinet Apothecary: Natural Health at Your Fingertips"
EBook Entrepreneur: Crafting Your Path to Profit
The Writer's Odyssey: Crafting Your Literary Legacy, A New Writer's Guide Book
From Words To Wealth: Mastering Freelance Writing
The Morning Elixir of Life: The History and Art of Coffee

Watch for more at https://rkrause45.wixsite.com/mysite.

Table of Contents

Introduction:
Setting Sail on Your E-book Entrepreneur Journey

Welcome, aspiring E-book Entrepreneur, to a world of limitless possibilities and boundless creativity!

In the digital age, the realm of E-books and publishing has undergone a profound transformation. E-books, once a novel concept, have become a powerful medium for sharing knowledge, storytelling, and, yes, building a profitable business. As you hold this E-book in your hands (or on your screen), you're embarking on a journey that could change your life and career forever.

The allure of the E-book Entrepreneurship is undeniable. Picture this: the freedom to write and publish your ideas, the ability to reach a global audience, and the potential to generate a steady stream of income—all from the comfort of your own home. It's a dream that has become a reality for many, and it can be yours too.

But like any journey, success in the world of E-book entrepreneurship isn't guaranteed. It requires dedication, knowledge, and a strategic approach. That's where this E-book comes in. We'll be your compass, guiding you through the uncharted waters of E-book creation and entrepreneurship.

Throughout the pages ahead, you'll discover the secrets to crafting compelling E-books, understanding your target audience, marketing your work effectively, and turning your passion for writing into a profitable venture. Whether you're a seasoned wordsmith or a newbie with a story to tell, there's something here for you.

But this isn't just a passive reading experience. It's an invitation to take action. As you journey through these chapters, consider how each piece of advice can be applied to your unique E-book venture. Imagine the possibilities, the stories waiting to be told, the knowledge ready to be shared, and the profits waiting to be earned.

Are you ready to embrace the E-book Entrepreneur within you? Are you prepared to set sail on this exciting journey, armed with the knowledge and tools you need to succeed? If your answer is a resounding "Yes!" then let's dive in, headfirst, into the world of E-book entrepreneurship.

Your adventure begins now, and the path to profits awaits. So, turn the page, and let's embark on this incredible voyage together!

Chapter 1:
Introduction to E-book Writing

Hey there, future E-book superstar! Welcome to the fantastic world of E-book writing, where your words have the power to pave the path to riches right from the comfort of your own writing nook.

Picture this: you, in your comfiest pajamas, sipping your favorite brew (coffee, tea, or maybe a hot cocoa with extra marshmallows), laptop in front of you, and your imagination set free like a wild stallion galloping across the plains of creativity. This, my friend, is the enchanting realm of E-book writing.

But before we dive headfirst into this adventure, let's set the stage. E-books, as you may know, are those nifty digital E-books you can read on your tablet, Kindle, or even your good old smart phone. And guess what? People all around the globe are gobbling them up like candy at a carnival.

Now, you might be wondering, "Why should I even consider writing E-books?" Well, here's the juicy part: it's not just about the thrill of putting words on a virtual page. Nope, it's about something much sweeter - those elusive E-book riches!

E-book riches, my friend, are the golden nuggets that await talented writers like you in this digital treasure trove. It's the satisfaction of knowing that your words can entertain, educate, and even change lives. And yes, it's also about making some moolah while doing what you love.

So, what's in store for you in this chapter? Well, grab another cup of that delightful beverage because we're about to embark on this journey together.

Defining the E-book Landscape

First things first, let's set the stage. What exactly are E-books? Imagine a regular, old-fashioned E-book – you know the kind with pages you can touch. Now, shrink it down and digitize it. Voilà! You've got an E-book.

E-books come in various formats, like PDFs, EPUBs, and MOBIs, and they're perfect for reading on all your devices. Gone are the days of lugging around heavy tomes; with Ebooks, your entire library fits right in your pocket.

The Allure of E-book Riches

Now, here's the real head-turner. E-books have taken the reading world by storm. People are devouring them like they're the last piece of chocolate cake on Earth. And guess what? They're willing to pay for them!

Imagine this: you create a masterpiece, a E-book filled with your thoughts, stories, and expertise. You put it out there, and people from across the globe can buy it with just a click. You're not limited by the shelves of a physical Ebookstore. The world is your oyster, and it's just waiting for you to shuck it open.

And let's not forget the magic of passive income. Once your E-book is out there, it can keep earning for you while you sleep, sip margaritas by the beach, or even write your next masterpiece.

A Roadmap to Success

Now that you've got a taste of the E-book-writing dream, let's talk about what lies ahead. This E-book is your trusty roadmap, your guiding star, and your cheerleader rolled into one. It's going to take you by the hand and lead you through the wild and wonderful world of E-book writing.

We'll explore everything from setting up your perfect writing space to crafting captivating introductions, from navigating the maze of self-publishing platforms to marketing your E-book like a pro. By the time we're done, you'll be well on your way to E-book stardom.

But here's the thing: while we've got the roadmap, you're the driver. Your passion, creativity, and determination are the fuel that will power this journey. So, buckle up, my friend, because the adventure of a lifetime awaits you.

In the chapters to come, we'll dive deeper into each aspect of E-book writing. We'll uncover the secrets of research, choose the perfect topics, and draft your E-book with style and flair. We'll explore the exciting world of self-publishing and unveil the art of marketing. We'll even chat about dealing with feedback and reviews – because every writer faces those ups and downs.

But for now, take a moment to savor the idea that you're about to embark on a quest that could change your life. E-book writing isn't just about making money (though that's a sweet bonus); it's about sharing your unique voice with the world, leaving your mark, and, who knows, maybe even inspiring others.

So, sip that beverage, get comfy in your writing spot, and let's begin this journey together. It's time to turn your writing dreams into reality, my fellow E-book explorer.

Chapter 2:
Preparing Your Writing Space

Hey there, fellow wordsmith! It's time to talk about your writing lair, your creative sanctuary, the place where all the magic is going to happen - your very own writing space.

Imagine this: you, in your writing haven, surrounded by everything that inspires you. Whether it's a corner of your bedroom, a cozy nook in your living room, or even a converted closet, your writing space is where the E-book-writing adventure truly begins.

Creating an Inspiring Workspace

Let's start with the basics. Your writing space should be a haven of inspiration, a place where creativity flows like a river. It doesn't need to be a grandiose office; it just needs to be your special place.

⬦ **The Right Furniture:** Begin with a comfortable chair and a sturdy desk. Your back will thank you later for investing in a good chair. And make sure the desk has enough space for your laptop or computer.

⬦ **Ergonomics:** Pay attention to ergonomics. Your posture matters! Adjust your chair and screen to the right height so you can write comfortably for hours.

⬦ **Good Lighting:** Natural light is a writer's best friend, but if that's not possible, invest in bright, adjustable lighting. Your eyes will appreciate it.

⬦ **Personal Touch:** Add personal touches to make it your own. Maybe it's a potted plant, a motivational poster, or a collection of quirky knick-knacks. Surround yourself with things that make you smile.

Necessary Tools and Software

Now that your space is shaping up, let's talk about the tools of the trade. Here's what you need:

⬦ **A Reliable Computer:** If you're reading this, you probably already have one. Make sure it's in good working condition.

⬦ **Writing Software:** Microsoft Word, Google Docs, Scrivener, or any writing software you prefer. Find the one that suits your style and stick with it.

⬦ **Internet Connection:** A stable internet connection is essential for research, reference, and, of course, sending your masterpiece into the world.

⬦ **Notebooks and Pens:** Sometimes, inspiration strikes when you least expect it. Keep a notebook and pen handy for those brilliant ideas that pop up during dinner or while you're brushing your teeth.

Organization for Productivity

Now, let's tackle the big one: organization. A well-organized writing space can make or break your productivity. Here's how to keep your ideas flowing smoothly:

⬦ **Filing System:** Set up a filing system for your digital documents. Create folders for each project, research materials, and reference documents. Keep things tidy and easy to find.

◇ **Daily Routine:** Establish a writing routine that works for you. Some writers thrive in the early morning, while others are night owls. Find your groove and stick to it.

◇ **To-Do Lists:** Make daily to-do lists. Nothing beats the satisfaction of crossing off tasks. It keeps you focused and on track.

◇ **Minimize Distractions:** Identify distractions in your workspace and minimize them. Turn off social media notifications, close unnecessary tabs, and let your loved ones know when you're in writing mode.

◇ **Backup System:** Always have a reliable backup system in place. You wouldn't want to lose your precious work to a computer glitch.

◇ **Inspiration Board:** Consider creating an inspiration board with pictures, quotes, or images related to your current project. It can serve as a visual motivator.

◇ **Comfort Essentials:** Don't forget the essentials for comfort. Keep a cozy blanket for chilly days and a bottle of water to stay hydrated during those writing marathons.

Personalize Your Space for Inspiration

Remember, your writing space is a reflection of you. It's where your creativity takes flight, and your ideas come to life. So, personalize it to inspire yourself daily.

◈ **Photos and Mementos:** Display photos of loved ones or cherished memories. These little reminders can lift your spirits during tough writing days.

◈ **Aromatherapy:** Consider adding a diffuser with your favorite essential oils. Aromatherapy can help create a calming or energizing atmosphere, depending on your needs.

◈ **Background Music:** Create a playlist of your favorite tunes to set the mood. Some writers prefer total silence, while others thrive with background music.

◈ **E-books:** A shelf of your favorite E-books can be a wonderful source of inspiration. Pick up a E-book for a quick dose of motivation or to spark your creativity.

◈ **Motivational Quotes:** Place motivational quotes where you can see them. A well-placed quote can remind you why you started this journey in the first place.

Your writing space is more than just furniture and technology; it's your creative cocoon. Make it a place where you feel inspired, motivated, and ready to conquer the E-book-writing world.

Now that your writing space is prepped and primed, it's time to move on to the next chapter: researching like a pro. Get ready to dive deep into your chosen topics and uncover the gems that will make your E-book shine.

Chapter 3:
The Research Phase

Ahoy, aspiring scribe! Today, we're diving into the marvelous world of research, where the seeds of your E-book take root and blossom into captivating content. Think of research as the treasure hunt before the adventure – it's where you unearth the gems that will make your E-book shine brighter than a pirate's chest of gold doubloons.

Mastering the Art of Research

First things first, let's talk about what research really means in the E-book game. Research isn't just Googling stuff (though that's part of it), it's about becoming an expert in your chosen topic. Whether you're writing about quantum physics or the history of garden gnomes, research is your trusty guide through uncharted territory.

⬦ **The Internet is Your Friend:** Start by delving into the depths of the internet. Websites, blogs, and academic journals – it's all there waiting for you. But remember, not everything online is reliable. Stick to trusted sources.

⬦ **E-books, E-books, E-books:** Libraries, both physical and digital, are like treasure troves. Don your explorers' hat and dig deep into E-books related to your topic. You'll uncover hidden gems of knowledge.

⬦ **Interviews and Experts:** Reach out to experts in your field. You'd be surprised how willing many experts are to share their wisdom. Conduct interviews, attend conferences, and tap into their insights.

◈ **Document Everything:** Keep meticulous notes. Think of yourself as a detective, collecting clues. You'll need these notes later when you're weaving your narrative.

◈ **Cite Your Sources:** This is crucial! Whenever you use someone else's work, give credit where it's due. Not only is it ethical, but it also adds credibility to your writing.

Identifying Profitable E-book Niches

Now, let's chat about choosing the right niche for your E-book. A niche is like your E-book's secret hideout. It's the specific topic you're going to explore in-depth. Finding the right one is key to attracting eager readers.

◈ **Passion Meets Demand:** Your niche should be a sweet spot where your passion meets market demand. It's great to write about what you love, but make sure people want to read about it too.

◈ **Research the Market:** Take a peek at what's already out there. Are there E-books similar to your idea? If yes, that's a good sign – it means there's a market for it. But don't be afraid to put your unique spin on things.

◈ **Check Trends:** Keep an eye on trends. What's hot right now? Topics that are currently trending can be a goldmine if you catch the wave at the right time.

Analyzing Market Trends and Reader Preferences

Now, let's talk about staying ahead of the curve. Markets change, and reader preferences evolve. You want to be the E-book writer who anticipates those changes and rides the trends like a pro surfer catching the perfect wave.

◈ **Google Trends:** Google Trends is your crystal ball. It tells you what people are searching for online. Use it to gauge the interest in your chosen niche.

◈ **Social Media Buzz:** Social media can be your secret spy network. Join forums and groups related to your topic. What questions are people asking? What are they excited about?

◈ **Reader Surveys:** If you've got a fan base or an audience, ask them directly! Conduct surveys or polls to understand what your readers are hungry for.

◈ **Stay Agile:** Be ready to pivot. If you see a shift in trends or reader preferences, don't be afraid to adjust your sails. Flexibility can keep your E-books fresh and appealing.

So, there you have it, dear writer. Research is your compass, your treasure map, and your secret weapon. It's what sets your E-book apart from the rest. Dive into it like a fearless explorer, and remember, the more you know, the better your E-book will be.

In our next chapter, we'll talk about choosing the perfect topic for your E-book. It's like picking the juiciest fruit from the tree, and we'll show you how to do it like a pro. Until then, happy researching!

Chapter 4:
Choosing Profitable E-book Topics

Hey there, E-book enthusiast! Now that we've mastered the art of research in the previous chapter, it's time to dive headfirst into the thrilling world of topic selection. Imagine this chapter as a menu at your favorite restaurant, and you get to pick the most delectable dish to serve your readers. Let's get started!

Balancing Passion and Market Demand

Choosing the right E-book topic is like finding the perfect recipe for a dish you can't wait to share. You want to write about something you're passionate about, but you also need to ensure there's a hungry audience out there.

⬦ **Passion Project:** Start by listing your passions, interests, and areas of expertise. What gets your heart racing? Your E-book should be something you enjoy writing about, as it will shine through in your words.

⬦ **Market Demand:** Research your chosen topics to see if there's a demand for them. Are people searching for information or stories related to your passion? Google, Amazon, and other search engines can be your trusty companions in this quest.

⬦ **The Sweet Spot:** Ideally, you want to find the sweet spot where your passion intersects with market demand. It's like creating the perfect dish that's both tasty and in high demand.

Techniques for Generating Topic Ideas

Now, let's tackle the topic brainstorming process. It's like a chef experimenting with ingredients to create a masterpiece. Here are some techniques to fire up your creative stove:

◇ **Mind Mapping:** Grab a piece of paper, write your main topic in the center, and start branching out with related subtopics. It's like creating a visual buffet of ideas.

◇ **Keyword Research:** Use tools like Google Keyword Planner to discover popular search terms related to your passion. This can lead you to untapped niche ideas.

◇ **Ask Your Audience:** If you have a blog, social media following, or even friends and family who are interested in your writing, ask them what topics they'd love to read about.

◇ **Follow Trends:** Keep your finger on the pulse of current events and trends. Is there a hot topic you can spin into an E-book?

◇ **Solve Problems:** Think about common problems or questions within your passion. Creating an E-book that offers solutions or answers can be a winner.

The Art of Niche Selection

Alright, now let's talk about niches. A niche is like a unique spice blend that makes your dish stand out. It's your chance to carve a special place for your E-book in the literary world.

◇ **Narrow Down:** Instead of writing a general E-book about a broad topic, consider narrowing it down. For example, instead of "Travel," you could choose "Solo Backpacking Adventures in Southeast Asia."

◈ **Specialize:** Become an expert in your chosen niche. Dive deep, uncover hidden gems, and share insights that only an expert would know.

◈ **Check Competition:** Don't shy away from niches with competition. It means there's a demand, but strive to offer something different, unique, or better.

◈ **Personal Connection:** A niche that you have a personal connection to can be incredibly powerful. Your genuine passion will shine through your words.

Research the Market, Know Your Readers

Now, we're getting into the nitty-gritty of market research. It's like conducting taste tests to know exactly what your readers crave.

◈ **Know Your Audience:** Who are your potential readers? What are their preferences, interests, and pain points? Understanding your audience is key.

◈ **Competitor Analysis:** Take a peek at E-books similar to your potential topic. What's working for them? What can you do differently or better?

◈ **Keyword Research (Again):** Go back to keyword research, but this time focus on long-tail keywords. These are specific phrases that can help you target your niche.

◈ **Market Gaps:** Identify gaps in the market. Are there topics related to your passion that haven't been covered adequately? This could be your golden ticket.

The Final Decision

Now comes the exciting part – making the final decision. It's like putting the finishing touches on your masterpiece.

◈ **Trust Your Gut:** After all your research and brainstorming, trust your instincts. Which topic resonates with you the most? Which one excites you to write about?

◈ **Check Feasibility:** Assess the feasibility of your chosen topic. Do you have access to the resources and information needed to create a compelling E-book?

◈ **Plan Your Approach:** Outline your E-books' structure and chapters. This will give you a roadmap for your writing journey.

So there you have it, my fellow E-book explorer! Choosing the right topic is like selecting the perfect canvas for your masterpiece. Remember, it's a blend of passion, market demand, and a pinch of uniqueness that will make your E-book a must-read.

In our next chapter, we'll delve into the exciting world of planning your E-book project. It's time to roll up your sleeves, sharpen your pencils, and get ready to craft your literary gem. Until then, keep those creative fires burning!

Chapter 5:
Planning Your E-book Project

Hello, fellow writer extraordinaire! In this chapter, we're going to tackle one of the most crucial phases of your E-book-writing journey: planning. Think of this as the architectural blueprint for your literary masterpiece. Let's roll up our sleeves and dive into the art of project planning.

Creating a Realistic Project Plan

Imagine your E-book project as a grand adventure. Just like any daring expedition, it requires careful planning and preparation. A project plan is like your treasure map, guiding you through uncharted waters.

◇ **Set Clear Goals:** Begin by defining your E-books' objectives. Are you writing to educate, entertain, or inspire? What's the message or story you want to convey?

◇ **Establish Deadlines:** Set realistic deadlines for each phase of your project, from research to final edits. Having a timeline keeps you accountable.

◇ **Budget Your Time:** Allocate specific time slots for your writing. Whether it's an hour a day or a weekend marathon, consistency is key.

◇ **Track Progress:** Create milestones to track your progress. Celebrate each small victory on your way to completing the E-book.

Setting Achievable Goals

Now, let's talk about goals. Goals are like the stars in your writing sky – they guide you forward and keep you on track.

⟡ **SMART Goals:** Make your goals Specific, Measurable, Achievable, Relevant, and Time-bound. This way, you'll know exactly what you're aiming for and when you've achieved it.

⟡ **Break It Down:** Divide your project into manageable tasks. Instead of "Write Ebook," break it into chapters or sections. It makes the process less daunting.

⟡ **Prioritize:** Not all tasks are equal. Prioritize them based on importance and deadlines. Tackling high-priority tasks first gives you a sense of accomplishment.

Outlining Your E-books' Structure

Think of your E-books' structure as the framework of a building. It's what holds everything together and ensures a smooth reading experience for your audience.

⟡ **Table of Contents:** Start by creating a table of contents. This is like the roadmap for your readers, showing them what to expect.

⟡ **Chapter Breakdown:** Outline the content of each chapter. What specific topics will you cover? What's the logical flow from one chapter to the next?

⟡ **Introduction and Conclusion:** Pay special attention to your E-books' introduction and conclusion. The introduction should grab your readers' attention, and the conclusion should leave them satisfied or eager for more.

The Art of Research and Note-Taking

Now, let's talk about research again, but this time it's research with a twist – research tailored to your E-books' structure.

⬦ **Organize Your Research:** Review your research notes and organize them according to your E-books' chapters. This way, you can easily reference your sources when writing.

⬦ **Cite as You Go:** When you gather information, make sure to note down the sources. Proper citation is essential for maintaining credibility.

⬦ **Fill in the Gaps:** Identify any gaps in your research. Are there areas where you need more information or additional sources? Address these gaps before you start writing.

Character Development (If Applicable)

If your E-book involves characters, whether they're fictional or real people, it's crucial to develop them thoroughly. Characters are like the heart and soul of your story.

⬦ **Character Profiles:** Create detailed profiles for each character. Include their background, personality traits, motivations, and arcs if applicable.

⬦ **Character Relationships:** Think about how your characters interact with each other. How do their relationships drive the plot or convey your message?

Dialogue and Narrative (If Applicable)

If your E-book includes dialogue or a narrative, consider how these elements will play out.

◈ **Dialogue Flow:** Plan the conversations between your characters. Make sure they serve a purpose, whether it's to reveal information, develop relationships, or create tension.

◈ **Narrative Voice:** Decide on the narrative voice. Will you tell the story from a first-person perspective, third-person perspective, or multiple perspectives?

Visual Elements (If Applicable)

If your E-book includes images, illustrations, or other visual elements, think about how they'll fit into your structure.

◈ **Image Placement:** Determine where in the text these visuals will appear. They should enhance the content, not distract from it.

◈ **Permissions:** If you're using images or illustrations that aren't your own, make sure you have the necessary permissions or licenses.

The Final Project Plan

Now that you've covered all the elements of planning, it's time to consolidate everything into your final project plan. This document should be your go-to resource throughout your Ebook-writing journey.

◈ **Document Everything:** Your project plan should include your goals, deadlines, budgeted time, chapter outlines, character profiles, dialogue, and visual elements, if applicable.

◈ **Share Your Plan:** If you're working with others, such as an editor or a designer, share your project plan with them. Clear communication is key to a successful project.

◈ **Stay Flexible:** While a plan is essential, be prepared to adjust it as needed. Sometimes, inspiration strikes, and you might want to deviate from the plan slightly.

With your project plan in hand, you're now armed and ready to embark on your E-book-writing adventure. It's like having a trusty compass that will lead you to your literary destination. In the next chapter, we'll dive deep into the creative process of writing. Get your pens and keyboards ready – it's time to bring your E-book to life!

Chapter 6:
Writing with Creativity and Authenticity

Ahoy, creative soul! Now that we've laid the groundwork in the previous chapters, it's time to dive headfirst into the sea of creativity and authenticity. Writing is where the magic happens, where your words come alive, and your E-book begins to take shape. Grab your literary compass and let's set sail!

Infusing Your Unique Voice into Your Writing

Imagine your writing as a canvas, and your voice as the brushstroke that adds personality, color, and life to your masterpiece. Your voice is what makes your E-book distinctively you, and it's something your readers will treasure.

◈ **What's Your Flavor?** Take a moment to think about your writing style. Are you witty, serious, poetic, or casual? Your voice should reflect your personality and resonate with your target audience.

◈ **Authenticity Matters:** Be genuine. Readers can spot insincerity from miles away. Write from your heart, share your experiences, and don't be afraid to show vulnerability.

◈ **Engage with Emotion:** Touch your readers' hearts by evoking emotions. Whether it's laughter, tears, or a sense of wonder, emotions create a connection that keeps readers coming back for more.

The Power of Storytelling in E-books

Stories are like the secret ingredient that turns a good E-book into a page-turner. Stories engage, captivate, and make complex ideas relatable. So, let's dive into the art of storytelling.

◇ **Character Arcs:** If your E-book involves characters, make sure they undergo some form of transformation. It could be a change in mindset, behavior, or circumstance. Readers love to see characters evolve.

◇ **Conflict and Resolution:** Every good story has conflict. It's what keeps readers hooked. Create challenges and obstacles for your characters, and then provide satisfying resolutions.

◇ **Show, Don't Tell:** Instead of telling your readers something outright, show it through actions, dialogues, and sensory details. Let readers experience your story as if they're right there.

Captivating Your Readers with Engaging Content

Now, let's talk about keeping your readers glued to your E-book. It's like a mesmerizing dance where you lead, and they follow.

◇ **Hook Them from the Start:** Your first chapter should be a hook that reels readers in. It could be an intriguing question, a shocking statement, or a vivid scene.

◇ **Maintain Flow:** Ensure a smooth flow from chapter to chapter. Think of it as a river where each chapter is a bend leading to the next adventure. No sudden drops or stagnant pools.

◈ **Balance Information and Readability:** If your E-book is informational, strike a balance between providing valuable insights and making it readable. Avoid overwhelming readers with data dumps.

◈ **Cliffhangers and Transitions:** Use cliffhangers or transitions at the end of chapters to keep readers eager to turn the page. Make them wonder, "What happens next?"

Writing with Heart and Soul

Writing an E-book isn't just about transferring information from your brain to the page. It's about pouring your heart and soul into your words. It's about crafting a piece of art that leaves a lasting impression.

◈ **Passion Fuels Words:** When you're passionate about your topic, it shines through in your writing. Your enthusiasm is infectious and draws readers into your world.

◈ **Be Fearless:** Don't be afraid to take risks with your writing. Experiment with different styles, narrative techniques, or even unconventional structures if it serves your story.

◈ **Perseverance is Key:** Writing can be tough at times. There will be moments when you doubt your abilities or face writer's block. Persevere through these challenges – every writer does.

◈ **Editing is Your Ally:** Your first draft is like a rough sculpture. Editing is where you refine, polish, and chisel away the excess to reveal the masterpiece within.

Write Like Nobody's Watching

Imagine you're writing in a cozy, soundproof room where no one is watching. This freedom allows you to write without self-judgment, to explore new ideas, and to be your authentic self.

⬧ **The First Draft:** Write your first draft as if no one will ever read it. Pour your thoughts onto the page without worrying about perfection.

⬧ **Silence the Inner Critic:** That little voice in your head that whispers, "Is this good enough?" Silence it for now. You can invite it back during the editing phase.

⬧ **Create a Writing Ritual:** Develop a writing ritual or habit that helps you get into the creative zone. It could be lighting a scented candle, playing soft music, or even wearing your lucky socks.

⬧ **Share Your Passion:** Remember why you started writing this E-book in the first place. Let your passion fuel your words, and it will shine through in your writing.

As you embark on this creative journey, remember that your E-book is a reflection of you, your experiences, and your unique perspective. Be bold, be genuine, and let your creativity flow like a river. In the next chapter, we'll dive into the crucial phase of crafting a compelling introduction that will leave your readers eager for more. So, keep that creative fire burning, my fellow wordsmith!

Chapter 7:
Crafting a Captivating Introduction

Ahoy, fellow storyteller! In this chapter, we're going to unravel the art of crafting a captivating introduction for your E-book. Think of your introduction as the grand opening of a thrilling adventure, the moment when you invite readers to step into your world. Let's set the stage for an unforgettable journey.

The Power of First Impressions

Imagine your introduction as the first handshake with your readers. It's your chance to make a lasting impression and pique their curiosity. Here's how to do it like a pro:

◇ **An Intriguing Hook:** Start with a hook that grabs your readers' attention. It could be a fascinating fact, a thought-provoking question, or a vivid description. Make them want to read more.

◇ **Establish the Tone:** Your introduction sets the tone for the entire E-book. Whether it's serious, humorous, or heartfelt, ensure that the tone aligns with the E-books' overall theme.

◇ **Introduce the Promise:** Let your readers know what they can expect from your E-book. What valuable insights, stories, or knowledge will they gain? Create a sense of anticipation.

Connecting with Your Readers

Your introduction is also your chance to establish a connection with your readers. Think of it as extending a warm welcome to them. Here's how to make that connection:

◇ **Relatable Stories:** Share a personal anecdote or a relatable story related to your E-books' topic. It humanizes you as the author and draws readers in.

◇ **Speak Their Language:** Understand your target audience and speak their language. Use words and phrases that resonate with them and show that you understand their needs.

◇ **Ask Thoughtful Questions:** Pose questions that resonate with your readers' experiences or challenges. This encourages them to reflect and engage with your content.

Building Anticipation

Your introduction should be like the opening scene of a blockbuster movie, leaving your readers eager for more. Here's how to build anticipation:

◇ **Foreshadowing:** Hint at what's to come in your E-book. Tease the exciting or insightful moments readers can look forward to as they journey through your pages.

◇ **Mystery and Curiosity:** Create an element of mystery or curiosity. Pose questions that you'll answer later in the E-book, sparking curiosity and motivating readers to keep reading.

◇ **Promise of Transformation:** If your E-book is about personal development or self-help, promise readers a positive transformation. Let them know that by the end, they'll have new insights or skills.

The Length and Structure

The length of your introduction depends on the overall length of your E-book. However, as a general guideline, your introduction should be concise, typically ranging from one to a few pages. Keep it engaging and to the point.

◈ **Introduction Structure:** Your introduction can follow a structure similar to this:

1. **Hook:** Grab readers' attention.

2. **Personal Connection:** Share a personal story or relate to the readers.

3. **Promise:** Explain what your E-book will offer.

4. **Foreshadowing:** Give readers a taste of what's ahead.

Revising and Polishing

The first draft of your introduction is like a rough gemstone. It needs polishing to reveal its true brilliance. Here's how to revise and refine your introduction:

◈ **Read Aloud:** Read your introduction aloud. It helps you identify awkward sentences or phrases and ensures the flow is smooth.

◈ **Trim the Excess:** Remove any unnecessary details or repetitive information. Keep it focused on what's essential.

◇ **Seek Feedback:** Don't hesitate to share your introduction with beta readers, friends, or writing groups. Their feedback can provide valuable insights.

◇ **Check for Consistency:** Ensure that the tone and style of your introduction align with the rest of the E-book.

A Sneak Peek at Chapter 1

Sometimes, your introduction can segue seamlessly into the first chapter. It's like leaving a breadcrumb trail that leads your readers deeper into the story. Here's how to make that transition smooth:

◇ **Continuity:** Ensure that the tone, style, and content of your first chapter flow naturally from the introduction. It should feel like a seamless transition.

◇ **Reiterate the Promise:** Remind readers of the promise you made in the introduction. Let them know that the journey is about to begin.

◇ **Engage Immediately:** The first chapter should engage readers from the get-go. Start with an impactful scene or a compelling statement.

Your Introduction Checklist

Before you consider your introduction complete, go through this checklist to ensure it's as captivating as it can be:

◇ ☐ Does it have a hook that grabs readers' attention?

◇ ☐ Does it establish the tone of your E-book?

◇ ☐ Does it connect with your target audience?

◇ ☐ Does it build anticipation for what's to come?

◇ ☐ Is it concise and to the point?

◇ ☐ Have you read it aloud for clarity and flow?

◇ ☐ Have you sought feedback from others?

◇ ☐ Does it transition smoothly into the first chapter?

Your introduction is your E-books' front door, welcoming readers into a world of knowledge, adventure, or inspiration. Craft it with care, and you'll set the stage for a reading experience that leaves a lasting mark. In the next chapter, we'll delve into the meat of your E-book, where you'll dive deep into your chosen topic. Until then, happy writing, and may your introduction be as captivating as a siren's song!

Chapter 8:
Navigating the Writing Process

Ahoy, brave writer! In this chapter, we're going to sail through the intricate waters of the writing process. Think of it as charting a course for your E-book, navigating each wave of creativity, and steering toward your destination. So, hoist your literary sails, and let's begin this voyage!

The Writing Sanctuary

Imagine your writing space as your personal ship's cabin, a haven where inspiration flows freely. Here's how to create your writing sanctuary:

◈ **Clutter Be Gone:** Clear your workspace of distractions. A clutter-free zone enhances focus.

◈ **Comfort is Key:** Ensure your writing chair is comfy, your desk is at the right height, and your screen is well-lit. Your body should feel at ease so your mind can roam freely.

◈ **Inspiration Wall:** Surround yourself with sources of inspiration – quotes, images, or artwork that resonate with your E-books' theme.

◈ **Rituals:** Establish writing rituals. Whether it's a cup of tea, a lucky pen, or a specific playlist, rituals signal your brain that it's time to create.

Embracing the First Draft Adventure

Your first draft is like setting sail on an uncharted sea. It's exciting, unpredictable, and, at times, a little daunting. Here's how to embrace the adventure:

◈ **Set Realistic Goals:** Determine a daily or weekly word count goal. It keeps you on track without overwhelming you.

◈ **Silence the Inner Critic:** The first draft is not the time for self-judgment. Write without hesitation. You can refine later.

◈ **Write Like a Cyclone:** Let your thoughts flow like a stormy sea. Don't worry about perfection; you're collecting the raw materials for your masterpiece.

◈ **Pause for Inspiration:** If you hit a rough patch, take a break. Step outside, read a E-book, or simply breathe. Inspiration often strikes when you least expect it.

Navigating the Storm of Writer's Block

Writer's block can be like an unexpected squall on your writing journey. Here's how to navigate these stormy waters:

◈ **Change Scenery:** If you're stuck, move to a different location. A change of environment can stimulate creativity.

◈ **Free writing:** Write without a specific goal or structure. Let your thoughts flow freely, even if they seem unrelated to your E-book.

◈ **Writing Prompts:** Use writing prompts to kick start your creativity. They provide a direction when you're feeling lost.

◇ **Read for Inspiration:** Sometimes, reading E-books or articles related to your topic can reignite your passion and creativity.

The Art of Revision and Editing

Your first draft is like uncut gemstone, and revision is the process of shaping it into a sparkling jewel. Here's how to master this art:

◇ **Let It Rest:** After completing your first draft, put it aside for a while. This distance allows you to view it with fresh eyes during revision.

◇ **Big Picture Edits:** Begin with major revisions. Check if your E-book flows logically, if your arguments are coherent, and if your characters are well-developed.

◇ **Sentence-Level Edits:** Zoom in and edit sentence by sentence. Look for clarity, grammar, and style issues. It's the fine-tuning stage.

◇ **Peer Review:** Share your work with trusted peers or beta readers. Their feedback can uncover blind spots and offer valuable insights.

Polishing Your Prose

Imagine your writing as a ship's hull, smooth and sleek for efficient sailing. Here's how to polish your prose:

◇ **Eliminate Fluff:** Trim unnecessary words and phrases. Clear writing is powerful writing.

◇ **Varied Sentence Structure:** Mix up sentence lengths and structures. It keeps readers engaged.

◇ **Vivid Descriptions:** Use sensory details to paint a vivid picture. Make your readers feel like they're part of the story.

◇ **Dialogue Realism:** If your E-book includes dialogue, make it sound natural. Read it aloud to ensure it flows smoothly.

Seeking Feedback and Revisions

Seeking feedback is like getting a second mate's perspective on your course. Here's how to navigate this process:

◇ **Choose Wisely:** Select beta readers or writing peers who understand your E-books' genre and audience.

◇ **Feedback Questions:** Ask specific questions when seeking feedback. For example, inquire about character development, pacing, or clarity.

◇ **Embrace Critique:** Be open to constructive criticism. Feedback helps you improve your work.

◇ **Iterate and Revise:** Based on feedback, revise your E-book as needed. Sometimes, it takes several rounds of revision to reach your desired destination.

Proofreading and the Final Checks

The final leg of your journey is like approaching a safe harbor. But first, you must navigate the treacherous waters of proofreading and final checks:

◇ **Proofreading:** Check for spelling, grammar, and punctuation errors. Tools like grammar checkers can be helpful, but don't rely solely on them.

◈ **Consistency:** Ensure consistency in formatting, style, and terminology throughout your E-book.

◈ **Read Aloud:** Read your entire E-book aloud. It helps catch awkward sentences and ensures a smooth reading experience.

◈ **Formatting:** Format your E-book for readability. Ensure fonts, headings, and spacing are consistent.

◈ **Test Read:** Enlist a few trusted readers to test-read your E-book. They can catch any lingering issues.

The Finishing Touches

Just like a ship's captain hoisting the sails for the final journey, here are some finishing touches:

◈ **Title and Cover:** Ensure your E-book has an eye-catching title and an appealing cover. These elements are your ship's flag.

◈ **Copyright and Legal:** Confirm that you have the necessary rights for any quotes, images, or references used in your E-book.

◈ **Metadata:** Set the metadata for your E-book, including keywords and categories. This helps it reach the right audience.

◈ **Publishing Platform:** Choose a platform to publish your E-book, whether it's an online marketplace or your website.

◈ **Launch Plan:** Plan your E-books' launch strategy. This could include promotional activities, blog posts, or social media announcements.

The Journey's End

Congratulations, fearless writer! You've navigated the often tumultuous waters of the writing process and brought your E-book to fruition. As you prepare to set sail into the world of readers and share your literary treasure, remember that writing is an ongoing adventure. Embrace it, learn from each voyage, and keep honing your skills.

In the next chapter, we'll explore the exciting world of E-book publishing and marketing. It's time to prepare for the grand voyage ahead! Until then, may your pen be swift, and your creativity boundless.

Chapter 9:
Navigating the World of E-book Publishing and Marketing

Ahoy, savvy author! In this chapter, we're diving into the exciting world of E-book publishing and marketing. Think of it as setting sail into uncharted territories, spreading the word about your literary treasure, and ensuring it reaches the eager hands of readers. Ready to embark on this thrilling journey? Let's weigh anchor and cast off!

The Voyage of E-book Publishing

Publishing your E-book is like setting sail on a grand adventure, and the digital seas are waiting for you. Here's how to navigate this voyage:

◇ **Choosing Your Harbor:** Decide where you'll publish your E-book. Options include Amazon Kindle Direct Publishing, Apple E-books, Barnes & Noble Nook Press, and more. Each harbor has its own rules and guidelines, so familiarize yourself with them.

◇ **Formatting for E-readers:** Ensure your E-book is formatted correctly for various e-readers and devices. Each platform may have specific formatting requirements.

◇ **E-book Cover Art:** Invest in a professional E-book cover design. Your cover is your E-books' first impression, and it should be visually appealing and relevant to your content.

◇ **Pricing Strategy:** Decide on a pricing strategy. Will you offer your E-book for free, at a low price, or at a premium? Consider factors like your target audience and competition.

◈ **ISBN and Copyright:** Decide whether you want to obtain an ISBN (International Standard E-book Number) for your E-book. Additionally, make sure your E-book is protected by copyright.

Setting Your E-book Course: Marketing Strategy

Now that your E-book is ready to set sail, it's time to chart a course for success. Marketing is like plotting a course to guide readers to your literary treasure.

◈ **Know Your Readers:** Understand your target audience. What are their interests, needs, and preferences? Tailor your marketing efforts to reach them effectively.

◈ **Author Branding:** Build your author brand. This is like hoisting your unique flag in the literary world. Share your author story and connect with your audience on social media and your website.

◈ **Pre-Launch Buzz:** Create anticipation before your E-books' launch. Share sneak peeks, behind-the-scenes content, or even run a countdown to build excitement.

◈ **Leverage E-book Bloggers and Reviewers:** Reach out to E-book bloggers and reviewers in your genre. Offer them a free copy of your E-book in exchange for an honest review.

Anchoring in Social Media Harbor

Social media is like the bustling harbor where you can drop anchor to reach a broader audience. Here's how to make the most of it:

◈ **Choose the Right Platforms:** Focus on social media platforms where your target audience hangs out. It could be Face E-book, Twitter, Instagram, or even niche forums.

◈ **Engage Authentically:** Don't just promote your E-book; engage with your followers authentically. Share insights, respond to comments, and build a community.

◈ **Visual Appeal:** Use eye-catching visuals like E-book quotes, custom graphics, and images related to your E-book. Visual content tends to grab more attention.

◈ **Hashtags:** Use relevant hashtags to reach a broader audience. Research popular hashtags in your genre and incorporate them into your posts.

E-book Launch Party: Online and Offline

Launching your E-book is like throwing a grand celebration. Whether it's virtual or in-person, make it an event to remember:

◈ **Virtual Launch:** Host an online launch party on platforms like Facebook or Zoom. Invite friends, family, and readers. Share readings, Q&A sessions, and giveaways.

◈ **Offline Events:** If circumstances allow, consider organizing physical E-book launch events at local bookstores or community venues. These events can create a buzz and allow you to connect with readers face to face.

The Importance of Reviews and Ratings

Reviews and ratings are like the stars that guide future readers to your E-book. Here's how to encourage and manage them:

◇ **Request Reviews:** Reach out to your early readers, friends, and family to leave honest reviews on your chosen E-book platform. Positive reviews can attract more readers.

◇ **Engage with Reviewers:** Respond to reviews, both positive and critical, with gratitude and professionalism. It shows that you value your readers' opinions.

◇ **Avoid Fake Reviews:** Never, under any circumstances, create fake reviews or purchase them. It can damage your reputation and get you banned from E-book platforms.

Sailing the Seas of Promotion

Promotion is like setting sail to explore new territories. Here's how to promote your E-book effectively:

◇ **E-book Blog Tours:** Arrange virtual E-book blog tours. These tours involve various bloggers featuring your E-book on their blogs, which can generate buzz.

◇ **Paid Advertising:** Consider paid advertising on platforms like Amazon, Face E-book, or Good Reads. Set a budget and target your ads to reach your ideal readers.

◇ **Email Marketing:** Build an email list of interested readers. Send them updates about your E-book, exclusive content, or special offers.

Course Correction: Analyzing Results

After your E-book has been sailing for a while, it's crucial to assess your progress and make any necessary course corrections:

◈ **Sales and Downloads:** Keep track of your E-book sales and downloads. Analyze which marketing efforts are yielding the best results.

◈ **Reader Feedback:** Pay attention to reader feedback. Are there common themes in their reviews or comments that you can address in future E-books?

◈ **Social Media Analytics:** Use social media analytics tools to track engagement, click-through rates, and the effectiveness of your posts.

◈ **Ad Campaign Performance:** If you're running ad campaigns, monitor their performance. Adjust your strategy based on what's working.

The Ongoing Journey

Remember, your journey as an author doesn't end with one E-book. It's an ongoing adventure filled with new horizons, fresh ideas, and more stories to tell. Keep honing your craft, engaging with readers, and setting sail into the literary seas with each new project.

In the next chapter, we'll explore the rewards of your hard work and the satisfaction of reaching your destination as an E-book entrepreneur. Until then, may your marketing efforts be fruitful, and your literary ship sail on toward success!

Chapter 10:
The Rewards of Your E-book Entrepreneurship Journey

Ahoy, intrepid author-entrepreneur! In this chapter, we'll set anchor and reflect on the rewards and satisfaction that come from your journey as an E-book entrepreneur. Picture this as a serene harbor where you can bask in the warm sun of your accomplishments, surrounded by the literary treasures you've created. Let's dive into the fulfilling world of being an E-book entrepreneur.

The Fruit of Your Labors

Your E-book is like a treasure chest, and it's time to open it and appreciate the wealth of rewards inside:

◇ **Financial Rewards:** Successful E-book entrepreneurship can lead to a steady stream of income. With each sale, you reap the financial benefits of your hard work.

◇ **Freedom and Flexibility:** Being an E-book entrepreneur often means freedom and flexibility in your work schedule. You're the captain of your literary ship, setting your own course.

◇ **Global Reach:** E-books can be downloaded worldwide, giving you the opportunity to connect with readers from different corners of the globe. Your words can transcend borders.

Reader Connections

As an author, one of the most rewarding aspects is connecting with your readers:

◈ **Fan Letters:** Receiving heartfelt letters or messages from readers who were deeply moved or inspired by your E-book is a gratifying experience. Your words have touched their lives.

◈ **Engaging with Readers:** Interacting with readers on social media or through author events creates a sense of community. You can discuss your E-book, answer questions, and even share insights into your writing process.

◈ **Impactful Stories:** Readers may share stories of how your E-book made a positive impact on their lives. These stories can be heartwarming and motivating.

The Creative Satisfaction

Creating an E-book is a labor of love, and the satisfaction of seeing your ideas come to life is unparalleled:

◈ **Personal Growth:** Your journey as an E-book entrepreneur is a path of personal growth. You've honed your writing skills, marketing acumen, and entrepreneurial spirit.

◈ **Creative Outlet:** Writing and publishing E-books allow you to express your creativity. You can explore various genres, styles, and themes with each new project.

◈ **Legacy Building:** Your E-books are a part of your legacy. They'll continue to exist in the digital world, potentially touching readers for generations to come.

Building Your Author Brand

Becoming an E-book entrepreneur is a journey toward building your author brand:

◈ **Recognition:** Over time, your name can become synonymous with quality writing in your chosen genre or niche.

◈ **Trustworthiness:** As you consistently deliver valuable content, readers come to trust your expertise and rely on your E-books for reliable information or engaging stories.

◈ **Networking:** The journey often involves networking with fellow authors, industry professionals, and literary enthusiasts. These connections can open doors to new opportunities.

The Joy of Continued Writing

The end of one E-book journey is the beginning of the next. Writing is a passion that keeps giving:

◈ **New Adventures:** With each new E-book, you embark on a fresh adventure. You explore new topics, create new characters, and face new challenges.

◈ **Evolution as an Author:** You evolve as an author with each project. Your writing style matures, your storytelling deepens, and your creativity knows no bounds.

◈ **Legacy of Literature:** With each E-book you publish, you contribute to the world of literature. Your words become a part of the rich tapestry of human storytelling.

The Legacy You Leave

Think of your E-books as lighthouses, guiding readers through the seas of knowledge and imagination. Your legacy as an E-book entrepreneur is one of enlightenment and inspiration:

◇ **Educational Legacy:** If your E-books are educational or informative, you leave a legacy of knowledge that can empower and educate others.

◇ **Entertainment Legacy:** If your E-books entertain, you leave behind a legacy of joy and escape, giving readers a chance to immerse themselves in captivating worlds.

◇ **Inspirational Legacy:** If your E-books inspire, you leave a legacy of motivation and encouragement, helping others overcome obstacles and pursue their dreams.

A Heartfelt Thank You

Before we lower the anchor on this chapter, it's essential to express gratitude:

◇ **Readers:** Thank your readers for their support, feedback, and enthusiasm. Without them, your E-books would remain undiscovered treasures.

◇ **Fellow Authors:** Acknowledge the fellow authors, mentors, and writing communities that have been your companions on this voyage.

◇ **Family and Friends:** Show appreciation for the friends and family who have stood by you, cheering you on as you pursued your passion.

The Ongoing Odyssey

Being an E-book entrepreneur is an ongoing odyssey filled with endless possibilities. As you navigate the literary seas, continue to set sail with enthusiasm, embrace new challenges, and let your creativity shine.

Your journey as an E-book entrepreneur may have reached its destination for this chapter, but there are countless more stories to tell and readers to inspire. May your future voyages be as fulfilling and adventurous as this one.

And so, dear author-entrepreneur, as we sail into the sunset of this chapter, I raise a metaphorical toast to your remarkable journey. Here's to the rewards of your hard work, the connections you've made, and the endless horizons of your literary future.

Chapter 11:
The Craft of Compelling Characters

Ahoy there, fellow storyteller! In this chapter, we're diving deep into the art of crafting characters that leap off the page and into your readers' hearts. Imagine it as assembling a crew for your literary ship, each character with a unique role to play in your E-books' voyage. So, sharpen your character-creating skills and let's set sail!

Characters: The Heart of Your Story

Characters are like the North Star in the night sky of your narrative. They guide readers through your E-books' twists and turns, forging connections and evoking emotions. Here's how to craft characters that shine:

◇ **Character Depth:** Think of your characters as icebergs – what readers see on the surface is only a fraction of their true depth. Explore their pasts, fears, and desires to create complex, relatable characters.

◇ **Motivations:** What drives your characters? Are they seeking love, revenge, redemption, or a hidden treasure? Understanding their motivations shapes their actions and decisions.

◇ **Flaws and Virtues:** Imperfections make characters human. Give them flaws and virtues that add authenticity and readability.

Protagonists: The Heroes of Your Tale

Your protagonist is the captain of your literary ship, guiding readers through the narrative's highs and lows. Here's how to create a captivating hero:

⬦ **Goals and Obstacles:** Define clear goals for your protagonist. What do they want, and what's standing in their way? It's the essence of your E-books' conflict.

⬦ **Character Arc:** Consider the journey your hero will undertake. How will they evolve and grow throughout the story? A well-crafted character arc adds depth.

⬦ **Relatability:** Readers should see themselves, or at least a reflection, in your protagonist. Their struggles and triumphs should resonate.

Antagonists: The Storm on the Horizon

Every captivating story needs a formidable foe, a challenge for the protagonist to overcome. Crafting a memorable antagonist is like creating the perfect storm:

⬦ **Motivations and Justifications:** Antagonists aren't just evil for the sake of it. What drives their actions? They should believe their goals are just as valid as the hero's.

⬦ **Complexity:** Give your antagonist depth. Even if readers don't agree with their actions, they should understand their reasons on some level.

⬦ **Conflict Styles:** Explore the clash of personalities and ideologies between the protagonist and antagonist. It's where the story's tension lies.

Supporting Cast: The Crewmates

Your supporting characters are the loyal crewmates, each contributing to the narrative's success. Here's how to make them memorable:

⬦ **Roles and Functions:** Define the roles each supporting character plays in the story. Are they a mentor, a sidekick, or a love interest? Their functions should complement the protagonist's journey.

⬦ **Distinct Personalities:** Give each supporting character a unique personality, voice, and quirks. This diversity adds richness to your E-book.

⬦ **Backstories and Goals:** Like the protagonist, supporting characters have their own backstories and goals. These can intersect with or diverge from the hero's path, creating subplots.

Dialogue: The Ship's Communication

Dialogue is like the ship's communication system, enabling characters to interact and share their thoughts and emotions. Here's how to make it shine:

⬦ **Character Voices:** Each character should have a distinct voice. Consider their background, education, and personality when crafting their dialogue.

⬦ **Subtext:** Sometimes, what characters don't say is as important as what they do. Subtext adds depth and intrigue to conversations.

◇ **Conflict and Resolution:** Use dialogue to build tension and resolve conflicts. Sharp exchanges or heartfelt confessions can reveal character dynamics.

Show, Don't Tell: Painting Pictures with Words

Instead of telling readers about your characters, show them in action. It's like using a vivid painting to depict your characters' traits and emotions:

◇ **Body Language:** Describe characters' body language and gestures. Are they fidgety, confident, or slumping in defeat?

◇ **Actions:** What characters do speaks volumes about their personalities. Do they rush into danger or hesitate cautiously?

◇ **Thoughts and Feelings:** Dive into characters' thoughts and feelings. Let readers see the world through their eyes.

Character Development: The Hero's Journey

Characters should evolve throughout your E-book, much like a sailor gaining experience on a long voyage:

◇ **Challenges and Growth:** Present characters with challenges that force them to change, learn, or adapt. This growth keeps the narrative engaging.

◇ **Learning from Mistakes:** Characters should make mistakes. It humanizes them and provides opportunities for growth.

◇ **Transformation:** By the end, characters should be different from whom they were at the start. The journey should leave its mark.

The Crew's Chemistry: Interactions Matter

Characters' interactions are the currents that propel your story forward. Consider how they mesh or clash:

◇ **Relationship Dynamics:** Explore the dynamics between characters. Are they allies, rivals, or something more complex?

◇ **Conflict and Resolution:** Conflict between characters is a source of tension, while resolution can be satisfying. It's like the ebb and flow of the narrative tide.

◇ **Dialogue Tags:** Use tags like "he said" or "she exclaimed" sparingly. They should enhance, not distract from, the dialogue.

Character Consistency: Steady as She Goes

Maintaining consistency in character traits and behavior is like keeping the ship steady in rough waters:

◇ **Character Bibles:** Create character bibles with details about their appearances, personalities, and histories. It's a reference guide to ensure consistency.

◇ **Motivations and Goals:** Keep characters aligned with their motivations and goals. Sudden shifts should be deliberate and well-explained.

◈ **Evolution:** Characters can change, but these changes should be gradual and believable.

Reader Connection: The Destination

Ultimately, crafting compelling characters is about forging connections with your readers. When they care about your characters, they invest in your story:

◈ **Emotional Engagement:** Characters should evoke emotions – empathy, love, frustration – in your readers. This emotional connection keeps them turning the pages.

◈ **Relatability:** Readers should find something in your characters that resonates with their own experiences and emotions.

◈ **Character-Centric Plot:** Ensure that your plot is character-driven. Their actions and choices should shape the narrative.

Ready to Set Sail?

With these character-crafting skills in your writer's toolkit, you're well-prepared to navigate the intricate waters of storytelling. Characters are the compass that guides your narrative, and their journeys are the heart of your E-books' adventure.

In the next chapter, we'll delve into the captivating world of plot and pacing. It's time to plot your course, chart your narrative's twists and turns, and keep your readers hooked. Until then, may your characters be as vivid as the open sea, and your storytelling as compelling as the wind in your sails!

Chapter 12:
Navigating the Waters of Plot and Pacing

Ahoy, fellow wordsmith! In this chapter, we're venturing into the thrilling seas of plot and pacing. Think of it as setting your E-books' course, charting the narrative's twists and turns, and keeping your readers on the edge of their seats. So, hoist the sails, and let's dive into the art of storytelling!

Plot: The Map of Your Voyage

Plot is like the map that guides your literary ship through uncharted waters. Here's how to create a captivating one:

⬦ **Beginning, Middle, and End:** Every story has these three parts, but it's what happens within them that counts. The beginning hooks readers, the middle keeps them engaged, and the end delivers a satisfying resolution.

⬦ **Conflict and Tension:** Introduce conflict early on – it's the wind in your sails. It can be internal (emotional struggles) or external (adversaries, challenges).

⬦ **The Inciting Incident:** This is the event that sets your story in motion, the moment your protagonist can't ignore. Make it compelling, like the siren's call.

Character-Driven Plot: It's All About Choices

Your characters should steer the plot with their choices and actions. It's like letting the crew decide which islands to explore:

◈ **Goals and Obstacles:** Characters' goals drive the plot. Think of these as the treasures they seek. Obstacles are the storms they must navigate to reach them.

◈ **Decisions and Consequences:** Every choice characters make should have consequences, whether good or bad. It keeps the narrative dynamic.

◈ **Character Arcs:** As characters change and grow, so should the plot. Their evolution influences the story's direction.

Pacing: The Rhythm of Your Narrative

Pacing is the heartbeat of your story, determining how fast or slow your literary ship sails. Get it right, and you'll keep readers hooked:

◈ **Balance:** Mix action, dialogue, and introspection to create a balanced pace. It's like the rise and fall of waves – moments of tension followed by moments of respite.

◈ **Tension Building:** Increase tension before critical plot points. Build anticipation, like a brewing storm on the horizon.

◈ **Breathing Room:** Allow readers to catch their breath. Give them quiet moments to connect with characters and reflect.

Plot Structure: The Keel of Your Ship

A well-structured plot is like the keel of a ship, keeping it steady and on course. Explore these essential elements:

◇ **Introduction:** Set the stage, introduce characters, and establish the story's world.

◇ **Rising Action:** Build tension gradually, introducing obstacles and challenges.

◇ **Climax:** The story's most intense moment, where conflicts reach their peak. It's like a tempest at sea.

◇ **Falling Action:** After the climax, start tying up loose ends and resolving conflicts.

◇ **Conclusion:** Deliver a satisfying ending, like reaching a safe harbor. Readers should feel a sense of closure.

Subplots: Hidden Treasures in Your Story

Subplots are like hidden treasures waiting to be discovered. They add depth and complexity to your narrative:

◇ **Character-Specific Subplots:** Explore individual characters' personal journeys or challenges. It's like exploring secret islands in your story's archipelago.

◇ **Romantic Subplots:** Love and relationships can be engaging subplots. They add emotional depth and connect readers to characters on a personal level.

◇ **Parallel Storylines:** Introduce parallel storylines that intersect with the main plot. They can provide different perspectives and keep readers guessing.

Foreshadowing: Planting Clues along the Way

Foreshadowing is like leaving breadcrumbs for readers to follow. It adds mystery and intrigue:

◇ **Hints and Clues:** Drop subtle hints about future events or revelations. It's like whispers of an approaching storm.

◇ **Chekhov's Gun:** If you introduce a significant element, make sure it has a purpose later in the story. Readers will expect it.

◇ **Reader Engagement:** Foreshadowing engages readers, inviting them to speculate and anticipate what's coming next.

Twists and Surprises: Plot's Hidden Coves

Twists and surprises are like hidden coves in your narrative, waiting to be explored. They keep readers engaged and curious:

◇ **Reversals:** Turn expectations upside down. What seems like a calm sea can suddenly become a maelstrom.

◇ **Character Revelations:** Unveil hidden facets of your characters. It's like discovering a new island on your voyage.

◇ **Plot Swerves:** Take unexpected detours in the narrative. Surprise readers with sudden changes in direction.

Reader Engagement: The Ultimate Goal

The goal of your plot and pacing is to keep readers engaged from the first page to the last:

◈ **Hooks:** Start with a compelling hook that grabs readers' attention. It's like a lighthouse beckoning ships into a safe harbor.

◈ **Chapter Endings:** Each chapter should end with a cliffhanger or a question to entice readers to keep going.

◈ **Rhythm:** Create a rhythmic flow to your narrative. Just as waves rise and fall, so should the intensity of your story.

Editing and Revising: Navigating Rough Waters

After you've plotted your course and set sail, don't forget to navigate the editing and revision process:

◈ **Editing Passes:** Edit for grammar, spelling, and sentence structure. It's like fine-tuning your ship's engine.

◈ **Beta Readers:** Seek feedback from beta readers who can offer fresh perspectives on your plot and pacing.

◈ **Read Aloud:** Read your E-book aloud to yourself. It can help you identify pacing issues and awkward sentences.

A Voyage Well-Plotted

With a well-crafted plot and carefully considered pacing, your E-book is poised for a thrilling voyage. Just like a seasoned captain, you'll guide your readers through uncharted waters, surprising them with hidden treasures and captivating twists.

In the next chapter, we'll delve into the art of world-building and creating immersive settings. Get ready to explore new horizons and transport your readers to far-off lands! Until then, may your plot be as captivating as a siren's song, and your pacing as smooth as a steady breeze.

Chapter 13:

Crafting Immersive Settings and World-Building Wonders

Ahoy, fellow storyteller! In this chapter, we're embarking on a grand adventure to explore the art of world-building and creating immersive settings that transport your readers to distant realms. Think of it as charting uncharted lands, painting vivid landscapes, and inviting your readers to step into your literary world. So, grab your compass, and let's set sail into the realm of imagination!

Settings: The Canvas of Your Tale

Settings are like the canvas upon which your story unfolds. They shape the atmosphere, influence character actions, and breathe life into your narrative:

⬦ **Physical Details:** Describe the physical aspects of your setting – landscapes, buildings, weather, and time periods. It's like creating a portrait of the world.

⬦ **Sensory Details:** Engage readers' senses with descriptive language. Let them feel the cool breeze, taste the salty sea air, and hear the rustling leaves.

⬦ **Atmosphere:** Settings should convey an atmosphere that complements the story's mood. Is it eerie, cozy, bustling, or serene?

World-Building: The Architect of Imagination

World-building is the craft of constructing entire universes, whether they're fantastical realms or historical epochs. Here's how to build a world that captivates:

⬦ **Rules and Laws:** Define the rules that govern your world – physical laws, magical systems, and societal norms. It's like creating the framework of your universe.

⬦ **Cultures and Societies:** Develop distinct cultures, societies, and belief systems for your world's inhabitants. What do they value, and how do they interact?

⬦ **History and Lore:** Craft a rich history and mythology for your world. These tales can add depth and intrigue to your narrative.

Consistency: Keeping the World Steady

Maintaining consistency in your world-building is crucial, like keeping a ship steady in turbulent waters:

⬦ **Create a Bible:** Keep a world-building bible with details about your setting and its rules. It's your guide to staying on course.

⬦ **Research:** For historical or real-world settings, research is your anchor. Ensure accuracy in details like clothing, technology, and customs.

⬦ **Character Alignment:** Characters should be consistent with the world you've built. Their beliefs and actions should align with the setting.

The Setting as a Character: It Lives and Breathes

In some stories, the setting becomes a character in itself, influencing the plot and characters:

◇ **Personification:** Describe the setting as if it were alive. The sea could be a temperamental friend, and a forest, a silent observer.

◇ **Challenges and Rewards:** Settings can present challenges and offer rewards to characters. A harsh desert might test their survival skills, while a tranquil garden could offer solace.

◇ **Transformation:** Just as characters evolve, settings can change over the course of the story. A once-pristine forest might become tainted by dark magic.

The Power of Description: Paint with Words

Description is your brush, and words are the strokes that create your literary masterpiece:

◇ **Metaphors and Similes:** Use metaphors and similes to make descriptions vivid. The castle might stand like a sentinel, or the ocean could be as vast as eternity.

◇ **Show, Don't Tell:** Instead of telling readers about the setting, show it through characters' interactions, emotions, and observations.

◇ **Reader Immersion:** Invite readers to explore the setting through your characters' eyes. Let them experience it firsthand.

Unique Settings: Stand Out on the Map

Creating unique and memorable settings is like discovering uncharted islands:

⬦ **Unexpected Elements:** Add unexpected elements to your setting – a floating city, sentient plants, or a hidden dimension. Surprise your readers.

⬦ **Contrasts:** Create contrasts within your world. A bustling city might be surrounded by serene countryside, highlighting the differences.

⬦ **Symbolism:** Use setting elements symbolically. A decaying castle could represent a fallen dynasty, and a blooming garden, hope and renewal.

Setting-Driven Plot: The Journey

In some stories, the setting itself drives the plot. The journey becomes an exploration of the world:

⬦ **Travelogue Style:** Embrace a travelogue style of storytelling. Characters move through diverse settings, each with its own challenges and wonders.

⬦ **Discovery:** Characters can uncover secrets and mysteries within the setting itself. An ancient cave might hold forgotten treasures or perilous traps.

⬦ **World Exploration:** As characters explore, they learn about the world, its inhabitants, and its history. It's like peeling back the layers of an ancient map.

Setting and Genre: A Dynamic Duo

Different genres require different approaches to setting:

◈ **Fantasy Worlds:** In fantasy, you have the freedom to create entirely new worlds with magic, mythical creatures, and unique rules.

◈ **Historical Settings:** Historical fiction demands meticulous research to recreate past eras accurately.

◈ **Sci-Fi Landscapes:** Science fiction settings explore futuristic technology, alien worlds, and the impact of advanced science on society.

Reader Immersion: The Ultimate Goal

The goal of immersive settings and world-building is to transport readers to new horizons:

◈ **Reader Imagination:** Encourage readers to imagine themselves within the world you've created. Let them dream of embarking on their adventures.

◈ **Emotional Connection:** Make readers care about the setting. A well-crafted setting can evoke emotions and memories.

◈ **Reader Exploration:** Invite readers to explore your world's mysteries and hidden corners. Let them feel like intrepid adventurers.

Charting New Territories

With your newfound knowledge of world-building and setting creation, you're ready to chart new literary territories. Your settings will be more than backdrops; they'll be living, breathing elements of your story.

In the next chapter, we'll dive into the realm of dialogue and character interactions. It's time to give your characters voices and let them interact in ways that deepen your narrative. Until then, may your settings be as vast as the seven seas and as enchanting as the realms of dreams!

Chapter 14:
Mastering Dialogue and Character Interactions

Ahoy, storyteller extraordinaire! In this chapter, we're plunging into the captivating depths of dialogue and character interactions. Think of it as giving your characters voices that sing, creating conversations that sparkle, and bringing your narrative to life through the art of spoken words. So, gather 'round the virtual campfire, and let's embark on this thrilling leg of our literary journey!

Dialogue: The Heartbeat of Your Tale

Dialogue is like the heartbeat of your story, pulsing with life and energy. Here's how to make it beat strongly:

◇ **Character Voices:** Each character should have a distinct voice. Think of it as giving them their own musical instrument to play in the symphony of your story.

◇ **Diction and Vocabulary:** Consider a character's background, education, and personality when crafting their dialogue. A pirate's speech will differ from a scholar's.

◇ **Subtext:** Sometimes, what characters don't say is as important as what they do. Subtext adds layers of meaning and intrigue to conversations.

Effective Dialogue: It's More than Words

Dialogue isn't just about words; it's about the spaces between them. Here's how to make your exchanges compelling:

◈ **Show Character Traits:** Use dialogue to reveal character traits. Is a character verbose or terse, optimistic or cynical?

◈ **Conflict and Tension:** Conflict drives your story, and dialogue is a prime arena for it. Characters can spar with words just as they do with swords.

◈ **Plot Progression:** Dialogue should move the plot forward. It's like the current of a river, carrying your narrative along.

Realistic Dialogue: Eavesdrop on Life

Realistic dialogue mirrors the way people speak in real life. Eavesdrop on conversations and learn the rhythms of natural speech:

◈ **Pauses and Interruptions:** People don't always speak in complete, uninterrupted sentences. Pauses and interruptions add authenticity.

◈ **Body Language:** Describe characters' gestures and expressions during dialogue. Nonverbal cues can speak volumes.

◈ **Idioms and Slang:** Incorporate idiomatic expressions and slang if they fit the setting and characters. It adds flavor to your dialogue.

Taglines and Beats: Rhythms of Speech

Taglines (he said, she exclaimed) and beats (actions or descriptions within dialogue) help create rhythm in conversations:

◈ **Use Sparingly:** Taglines should be used sparingly to avoid repetition. Often, readers can infer the speaker from context.

◈ **Beats for Emphasis:** Use beats to emphasize actions or reactions during dialogue. They can enhance the scene's emotional impact.

◈ **Vary Sentence Length:** Mix short and long sentences in dialogue. It mimics the ebb and flow of natural conversation.

Subtext: The Unsaid and the Unseen

Subtext is like the hidden treasure beneath the waves. It's what characters don't say but convey through their words and actions:

◈ **Hidden Agendas:** Characters may have ulterior motives or secrets. These can create tension and intrigue in dialogue.

◈ **Emotional Depth:** Subtext adds emotional depth to conversations. A character's reluctance to discuss a topic can be as revealing as what they do say.

◈ **Character Relationships:** The dynamics between characters can be explored through subtext. It's like a dance of unspoken feelings.

Character Interactions: The Dance of Emotions

Character interactions are like a dance of emotions, where each step reveals something about the characters involved:

◈ **Conflict and Resolution:** Characters can clash, argue, and then reconcile. These interactions drive character development and plot progression.

◈ **Bonds and Friendships:** Show characters bonding, sharing moments of camaraderie, or offering support. These moments endear them to readers.

◈ **Romantic Relationships:** In romantic interactions, build chemistry, tension, and genuine connection. It's like a slow waltz towards love.

Dialogue and Character Growth: The Evolution

Characters should grow and change through their interactions. It's like a mirror reflecting their development:

◈ **Learning from Each Other:** Characters can learn valuable lessons from their interactions with others. It's a form of mutual growth.

◈ **Conflict as Catalyst:** Conflict in dialogue can force characters to confront their flaws or biases. It's a catalyst for change.

◈ **Evolution of Relationships:** As characters interact, their relationships should evolve. A rivalry might transform into respect, or a friendship into love.

Reader Engagement: The Ultimate Goal

The goal of compelling dialogue and character interactions is to engage readers on an emotional level:

◈ **Empathy:** Readers should empathize with characters and their struggles. Well-crafted dialogue can make readers care deeply.

◈ **Intrigue:** Engaging dialogue keeps readers turning pages to see what characters will say or do next.

◈ **Connection:** Readers should feel a connection to characters, as if they're part of their circle of friends or adversaries.

Editing Dialogue: Refining the Symphony

After the initial draft, edit and refine your dialogue:

◈ **Read Aloud:** Read your dialogue aloud to check for natural flow and rhythm. It helps identify awkward lines.

◈ **Cut the Excess:** Trim unnecessary dialogue that doesn't advance the plot or reveal character.

◈ **Beta Readers:** Seek feedback from beta readers to gauge the effectiveness of your dialogue.

Your Characters Speak

With these insights into dialogue and character interactions, your characters are ready to take the stage and speak their hearts and minds. Whether they're whispering secrets or shouting defiance, their voices will resonate with readers.

In the next chapter, we'll navigate the seas of conflict and tension, exploring how to create gripping conflicts that drive your story forward. Until then, may your character conversations be as lively as a bustling marketplace and your dialogue as rich as the tales told around a campfire under a starlit sky!

Chapter 15:
Crafting Gripping Conflicts and Tension

Ahoy, master of tales! In this chapter, we're setting sail into the tempestuous waters of conflicts and tension. Picture it as raising the Jolly Roger, letting your characters clash like thunder, and creating waves that keep your readers on the edge of their seats. So, hoist the anchor, and let's embark on this thrilling voyage through the art of storytelling's stormiest seas!

Conflict: The Raging Tempest of Narrative

Conflict is the raging tempest that propels your story forward. It's the push and pull, the clash of ambitions and desires that captivate readers:

⬦ **Types of Conflict:** There are several types of conflict, including character vs. character, character vs. self, character vs. nature, and character vs. society. Choose the one that best suits your story.

⬦ **External and Internal Conflict:** Characters wrestle not only with external foes but also with their inner demons, doubts, and desires.

⬦ **Goals and Obstacles:** Define clear goals for your characters, and then throw obstacles in their path. It's like setting sail toward treasure but facing treacherous waters.

Conflict-Driven Plot: Plot like a Hurricane

Conflict isn't just a part of your story; it is the story. Here's how to make it the hurricane that propels your narrative:

◈ **Escalation:** The conflict should escalate throughout the story, increasing tension and stakes. It's like the wind intensifying in a storm.

◈ **Character Motivations:** Characters' motivations should clash, creating the conflict. Their desires and values should be at odds.

◈ **Turning Points:** Define key turning points where conflicts reach their zenith. These moments should have profound consequences.

Creating Tension: Lightning in a Bottle

Tension is like lightning in a bottle – it electrifies your narrative and keeps readers on edge:

◈ **Foreshadowing:** Drop subtle hints and foreshadow events to come. It's like distant thunder announcing an approaching storm.

◈ **Uncertainty:** Keep readers guessing about the outcome. Uncertainty breeds tension.

◈ **Emotional Stakes:** Make sure there's something at stake that readers care about. Personal, emotional stakes intensify tension.

Dialogue in Conflict: Verbal Swordplay

Dialogue can be a battlefield where characters engage in verbal swordplay. Here's how to make it sharp and impactful:

◈ **Clashing Words:** Create verbal confrontations where characters challenge each other's beliefs, desires, or actions.

◇ **Subtext:** Use subtext to convey unspoken feelings and motives. What characters don't say can be as potent as what they do.

◇ **Escalation:** Dialogue in conflict should escalate, with characters becoming increasingly impassioned or desperate.

Character vs. Character: Duel of Wills

Character vs. character conflicts are like duels of wills, where personal motivations collide:

◇ **Antagonists and Protagonists:** Antagonists should be well-developed characters with their own motivations. They're not just obstacles but individuals with their own stories.

◇ **Character Development:** Conflict can drive character development. Characters evolve in response to challenges.

◇ **Moral Dilemmas:** Explore moral dilemmas where characters must choose between right and wrong, good and evil.

Character vs. Self: The Inner Battle

Character vs. self conflicts are the internal battles characters wage within themselves:

◇ **Inner Demons:** Characters grapple with inner demons, doubts, or conflicting desires. It adds depth to their struggles.

⬦ **Self-Discovery:** Character vs. self conflicts often lead to self-discovery and personal growth. Characters confront their flaws and limitations.

⬦ **Complexity:** Internal conflicts make characters relatable and human. Readers see themselves in these struggles.

Character vs. Nature: Surviving the Elements

In character vs. nature conflicts, characters face the raw power of the natural world:

⬦ **Survival:** Survival is often at stake. Characters must endure the elements, wildlife, or natural disasters.

⬦ **Nature as Metaphor:** Sometimes, nature serves as a metaphor for characters' internal struggles. A stormy sea can represent inner turmoil.

⬦ **Setting as Antagonist:** The setting itself can become an antagonist, with its own challenges and obstacles.

Character vs. Society: The Rebel's Cause

Character vs. society conflicts involves characters challenging the norms and rules of their world:

⬦ **Social Injustice:** Characters may rebel against oppressive systems, prejudices, or injustices. It's like lighting a revolutionary spark.

⬦ **Outsiders:** Characters who don't fit society's mold often become catalysts for change. They question the status quo.

◇ **Collateral Damage:** These conflicts can have consequences beyond the characters involved, affecting the entire society.

Resolving Conflict: Calm after the Storm

Every storm eventually passes, and so should your conflicts:

◇ **Resolution:** Conflict resolution provides closure to readers. It's the calm after the storm.

◇ **Character Arcs:** Characters should grow or change as a result of the conflicts they face. Their journeys should be transformative.

◇ **New Beginnings:** Sometimes, conflict resolution opens the door to new adventures or challenges. It's the promise of future stories.

Reader Engagement: The Ultimate Goal

The ultimate goal of crafting gripping conflicts and tension is to keep readers engaged, emotionally invested, and hungry for more:

◇ **Emotional Impact:** Well-executed conflict and tension can evoke strong emotions in readers, from suspense to empathy.

◇ **Page-Turning Power:** Tension keeps readers turning pages, eager to see how conflicts will unfold.

◇ **Character Connection:** Readers become more connected to characters as they witness their struggles and triumphs.

Plotting Your Narrative Storm

With these tools in hand, you're ready to plot your narrative storm, where conflicts rage like tempests and tension crackles like lightning. Your characters will be tested, your readers enthralled, and your story propelled to new heights.

In the next chapter, we'll explore the art of suspense and mystery, keeping your readers guessing and yearning for answers. Until then, may your conflicts be as fierce as a hurricane and your tension as electrifying as a lightning strike!

Chapter 16:
Weaving Suspense and Mystery into Your Narrative

Ahoy, intrepid scribe! In this chapter, we're delving deep into the captivating realm of suspense and mystery, where your readers become detectives, and your narrative becomes a labyrinth of secrets and surprises. Picture it as leaving tantalizing breadcrumbs, crafting enigmatic puzzles, and keeping your audience on the edge of their seats. So, light the lantern, and let's embark on this thrilling journey through the art of storytelling's shadowy alleys!

Suspense: The Art of Anticipation

Suspense is the art of anticipation, where readers eagerly await what comes next. Here's how to keep them on tenterhooks:

⬦ **Revealing Information:** Drip-feed information to readers, revealing just enough to pique their curiosity. It's like leading them deeper into the forest with each breadcrumb.

⬦ **Unanswered Questions:** Pose questions without immediate answers. Readers become invested in finding the solutions, like a mystery to be unraveled.

⬦ **Foreshadowing:** Foreshadow future events or revelations, creating a sense of impending doom or delight. It's the storm clouds gathering on the horizon.

Creating Mystery: The Puzzle Unfolds

Mystery is like a puzzle waiting to be solved. Here's how to craft one that keeps readers guessing:

◇ **The Enigma:** Introduce an enigmatic element early on, something unusual or unexplained. It's the locked door in a seemingly empty mansion.

◇ **Clues and Red Herrings:** Scatter clues throughout your narrative, but also toss in red herrings – false leads that confound readers. They're like mischievous spirits in the night.

◇ **Unveiling Secrets:** As the story progresses, gradually unveil the secrets and answers. It's like peeling back the layers of an onion.

Character Perspective: The Detective's Lens

Your characters become detectives, and their perspective is the lens through which readers investigate:

◇ **Limited Knowledge:** Characters often have limited knowledge, which mirrors readers' perspectives. They discover clues and information as the story unfolds.

◇ **Character Motives:** Explore characters' motives and desires. What do they want, and what are they willing to do to achieve it?

◇ **Unreliable Narrators:** Consider unreliable narrators who may misinterpret events or withhold information. They add layers of complexity.

Tension: The Breathless Moment

Tension is like the breathless moment when the noose tightens. Here's how to make your narrative pulse with it:

◈ **Timing:** Build tension through timing – the gradual increase of pressure, like a coiled spring.

◈ **Conflicts and Obstacles:** Introduce conflicts and obstacles that hinder characters' progress. It's like a maze of challenges.

◈ **High Stakes:** Make sure there's something significant at stake – a life, a secret, a cherished goal. Readers should care deeply about the outcome.

Dialogue in Mystery: Words Hold Secrets

Dialogue becomes a treasure trove of secrets and revelations in mystery narratives:

◈ **Cryptic Speech:** Characters may speak cryptically, dropping hints and clues in their conversations. It's like coded messages.

◈ **Misdirection:** Characters can use misdirection to divert attention from the truth. Their words are like veils concealing hidden truths.

◈ **Interrogations:** Interrogations and interviews can be riveting scenes where characters extract information or confront suspects.

Pacing: The Rhythm of Discovery

Pacing is like the rhythm of discovery – the ebb and flow of revelations and surprises:

⬦ **Climaxes and Lulls:** Alternate between climactic moments of revelation and quieter lulls where characters regroup or reflect.

⬦ **Revelations:** Each revelation should lead to new questions or mysteries. It's like a series of locked doors, each opening onto a new puzzle.

⬦ **Reader Engagement:** Keep readers engaged with a steady stream of discoveries. Don't let them linger too long without a new puzzle to solve.

Subplots and Twists: Uncharted Territories

Subplots and twists are like uncharted territories, waiting to be explored:

⬦ **Subplots:** Weave subplots into your narrative, each with its own mysteries and resolutions. They add depth and complexity.

⬦ **Twists:** Incorporate unexpected twists that upend readers' assumptions. It's like a sudden change in the wind's direction.

⬦ **Revealing Backstories:** Characters' backstories can hold the keys to the central mystery. Unveil them gradually to keep readers intrigued.

Resolving Mystery: The Light in the Darkness

Every mystery must eventually be solved. Here's how to reveal the truth:

◇ **Resolution:** Provide a satisfying resolution that ties up loose ends and answers lingering questions. It's like the dawn breaking after a long night.

◇ **Character Growth:** Show how characters have grown or changed as a result of their journey through mystery. It's the treasure they've gained.

◇ **Leave Open Doors:** While the central mystery is resolved, leave a few doors open for future adventures or unanswered questions.

Reader Engagement: The Ultimate Goal

The ultimate goal of suspense and mystery is to keep readers engaged, enthralled, and eager for more:

◇ **Curiosity:** Curiosity is the driving force. Make readers itch to uncover the truth.

◇ **Satisfaction:** A well-crafted mystery satisfies readers by providing answers and resolutions.

◇ **Longing for More:** Leave readers with a longing for more adventures and puzzles to solve.

Your Narrative's Shadows

With these techniques at your disposal, your narrative will become a labyrinth of shadows, where readers eagerly step into the darkness, armed with curiosity and a thirst for answers.

In the next chapter, we'll venture into the realm of emotions and character depth, where the heart of your story beats in every word and action. Until then, may your mysteries be as deep as the ocean and your suspense as thrilling as a midnight chase through the fog!

Chapter 17:
Evoking Emotions and Crafting Character Depth

Ahoy, storytelling virtuoso! In this chapter, we're diving deep into the mesmerizing depths of emotions and character depth, where your readers will experience joy, sorrow, and everything in between. Picture it as wielding the painter's brush, breathing life into your characters, and making your narrative a symphony of feelings. So, let the curtain rise, and let's embark on this exhilarating journey into the heart of storytelling!

Emotions: The Symphony of Human Experience

Emotions are the symphony of human experience, and your characters are the orchestra. Here's how to conduct their feelings:

⬥ **Range of Emotions:** Characters should experience a wide range of emotions, from love and happiness to anger and despair. It's like playing a full-scale concerto.

⬥ **Show, Don't Tell:** Instead of telling readers what characters feel, show it through their actions, thoughts, and dialogue. It's like a musical crescendo that swells from silence.

⬥ **Physical Manifestations:** Emotions often have physical manifestations. Characters might tremble with fear, flush with anger, or sigh with contentment.

Character Depth: The Art of Unveiling

Character depth is like peeling back the layers of an onion, revealing the complexities beneath the surface:

◈ **Backstories:** Create rich backstories for your characters, exploring their past experiences, traumas, and joys. It's like the overture that sets the tone.

◈ **Motivations:** Understand your characters' motivations – what drives them, what they desire, and what they fear. It's the melody that carries the narrative.

◈ **Flaws and Virtues:** Characters should have both flaws and virtues. These make them relatable and multi-dimensional, like harmonies and dissonances in music.

Empathy: The Bridge to Readers' Hearts

Empathy is the bridge that connects readers to your characters' emotions:

◈ **Inner Monologues:** Let readers into your characters' inner thoughts and feelings. It's like a soliloquy in a Shakespearean play.

◈ **Shared Experiences:** Create moments of shared experience between characters and readers. Readers should feel what characters feel, like an emotional duet.

◈ **Moral Dilemmas:** Explore moral dilemmas that resonate with readers. These dilemmas evoke empathy and introspection.

Character Arcs: The Journey of Transformation

Character arcs are like musical compositions, where characters undergo transformation:

⬦ **The Setup:** Introduce characters in their ordinary world, before the journey begins. It's the prelude to the main theme.

⬦ **The Conflict:** Characters face challenges and conflicts that force them to change. It's the tumultuous middle movement.

⬦ **The Resolution:** Characters emerge transformed, having learned and grown. It's the triumphant finale.

Relationships: The Harmony of Connections

Character relationships add harmony and discord to your narrative:

⬦ **Conflict in Relationships:** Conflict between characters can be as compelling as external conflict. It's the clash of instruments in a symphony.

⬦ **Bonds and Friendships:** Characters can form bonds and friendships that enrich their journeys. It's the duet that soothes the soul.

⬦ **Romantic Relationships:** Handle romantic relationships with depth and authenticity. Explore the challenges and joys of love, like a passionate love song.

Dialogue: The Music of Interaction

Dialogue is the music of character interaction, where emotions are played out:

◈ **Subtext:** Characters often don't say what they truly feel. Subtext adds depth to their conversations, like a hidden melody.

◈ **Conflict in Dialogue:** Dialogue can be a battleground of emotions, where characters confront each other's beliefs and desires. It's like a dramatic aria.

◈ **Revealing Emotions:** Use dialogue to reveal characters' emotions, whether through heartfelt confessions or heated arguments.

Setting and Atmosphere: The Stage for Emotions

The setting and atmosphere can enhance the emotional impact of your narrative:

◈ **Setting's Mood:** Choose settings that complement the emotions of the scene. A gloomy forest can intensify fear, while a sunlit meadow can enhance happiness.

◈ **Weather and Nature:** Use weather and nature to mirror characters' emotions. A storm can reflect turmoil, while a calm sea can signify peace.

◈ **Symbolism:** Employ symbolism in your setting. A decaying mansion can represent a character's inner struggles, while a blooming garden can signify hope.

Resonating with Readers: The Ultimate Goal

The ultimate goal of evoking emotions and crafting character depth is to create a symphony that resonates with readers:

◈ **Reader Empathy:** Make readers empathize with characters' journeys and emotions. Let them feel the highs and lows.

◈ **Investment:** Readers should be emotionally invested in the characters' fates. They should care deeply about what happens to them.

◈ **Reflection:** A well-crafted narrative leaves readers reflecting on their own lives and emotions, like the echoes of a poignant melody.

Your Characters' Hearts

With these techniques, your characters' hearts will beat in harmony with your narrative, and your readers will be moved by the symphony of emotions you orchestrate.

In the next chapter, we'll explore the art of tension and pacing, where you'll learn to keep your readers on the edge of their seats, eagerly turning pages to uncover the next twist. Until then, may your characters' emotions be as vivid as a rainbow after the storm, and your storytelling as soul-stirring as a timeless ballad!

Chapter 18:

Mastering Tension and Pacing for Page-Turning Suspense

Ahoy, tale-weaver extraordinaire! In this chapter, we're plunging headfirst into the captivating realms of tension and pacing. Picture it as a thrilling rollercoaster ride for your readers, where suspense builds, hearts race, and pages fly. So, fasten your literary seatbelt, and let's embark on this exhilarating journey through the art of storytelling's suspenseful twists and turns!

Tension: The Breathless Thrill Ride

Tension is the heartbeat of suspense, the pulse that keeps readers enthralled. Here's how to crank up the tension in your narrative:

⬦ **Rising Stakes:** Increase the stakes gradually. It's like climbing higher on a rollercoaster, with each turn becoming more intense.

⬦ **Foreshadowing:** Drop hints and foreshadow upcoming events to create anticipation. It's like the suspenseful music that cues danger in a movie.

⬦ **Unanswered Questions:** Pose questions without immediate answers. It's the mystery that keeps readers guessing.

Pacing: The Rhythm of Suspense

Pacing is the rhythm of suspense, the ebb and flow of excitement and calm. Here's how to master it:

◇ **Climaxes and Lulls:** Alternate between climactic moments of action and quieter lulls for character development or reflection. It's like the rollercoaster's drops and loops followed by serene stretches.

◇ **Short and Long Sentences:** Use short, rapid sentences during intense scenes to quicken the pace. Lengthen sentences during calmer moments. It's like the beat of a thrilling soundtrack.

◇ **Reader Engagement:** Keep readers engaged by maintaining a steady rhythm. Don't let them linger too long without something exciting happening.

Hooks and Cliffhangers: Keeping Readers on Edge

Hooks and cliffhangers are like bait for your readers, enticing them to keep turning pages:

◇ **Opening Hook:** Start with a compelling hook that grabs readers' attention. It's like the initial drop of the rollercoaster.

◇ **Chapter Endings:** End chapters with cliffhangers or unresolved questions. Readers won't be able to resist finding out what happens next.

◇ **Revelation Timing:** Reveal critical information at strategic points, creating "Aha!" moments for readers. It's like discovering a hidden path on a thrilling adventure.

Character Perspective: The Reader's Guide

Character perspective is your reader's guide through the suspenseful journey:

◇ **Limited Knowledge:** Characters often have limited knowledge, which mirrors readers' perspectives. They discover clues and unravel mysteries alongside readers.

◇ **Character Emotions:** Use characters' emotions to convey tension. When characters are anxious or fearful, readers will be too.

◇ **Unreliable Narrators:** Consider unreliable narrators who may misinterpret events, adding an extra layer of suspense.

Setting and Atmosphere: The Thrilling Backdrop

Setting and atmosphere can enhance the tension in your narrative:

◇ **Setting's Mood:** Use settings that complement the mood. A creepy, dimly lit forest can intensify fear, while a bustling city can amplify excitement.

◇ **Weather and Nature:** Employ weather and nature to create tension. A thunderstorm can enhance danger, while a serene, moonlit night can evoke romance.

◇ **Symbolism:** Symbolism in your setting can add depth. An abandoned, decaying mansion might symbolize decay or secrets.

Dialogue: The Verbal Showdown

Dialogue becomes a battleground for suspense, where words can be weapons:

⬦ **Verbal Conflict:** Use verbal conflicts to create tension. Characters can challenge each other's beliefs, reveal hidden motives, or express fear.

⬦ **Revealing Secrets:** Dialogue can be a vehicle for revealing crucial information. Characters might confess to crimes, disclose secrets, or confront long-buried truths.

⬦ **Timing:** Use dialogue timing to build suspense. Pauses or interruptions can leave readers hanging on every word.

Foreshadowing: The Art of Hints

Foreshadowing is like a trail of breadcrumbs leading readers deeper into the narrative:

⬦ **Subtle Hints:** Drop subtle hints early on about future events or revelations. Readers will be eager to see how they unfold.

⬦ **Recurring Motifs:** Use recurring motifs or symbols that hold significance. It's like an intricate puzzle waiting to be solved.

⬦ **Character Actions:** Characters' actions can foreshadow their intentions or future choices. Readers become detectives, piecing together the clues.

Resolving Tension: The Climactic Release

Every rollercoaster has its final descent, and so does your narrative. Here's how to resolve tension effectively:

◇ **Resolution:** Provide a satisfying resolution that ties up loose ends and answers lingering questions. It's like the moment of calm after a thrilling ride.

◇ **Character Growth:** Show how characters have grown or changed as a result of their suspenseful journey. It's the treasure they've gained.

◇ **Leave Open Doors:** While the main tension is resolved, leave a few doors open for future adventures or unanswered questions.

Reader Engagement: The Ultimate Goal

The ultimate goal of mastering tension and pacing is to keep readers on the edge of their seats, eagerly turning pages:

◇ **Excitement:** Keep readers excited and invested in the story's twists and turns.

◇ **Anticipation:** Make readers anticipate what's coming next, like a rollercoaster's next drop.

◇ **Satisfaction:** Ultimately, provide satisfaction by resolving tension and delivering a rewarding conclusion.

Your Suspenseful Symphony

With these techniques, your narrative will become a suspenseful symphony, where tension rises and falls, and readers are swept up in the excitement.

In the next chapter, we'll delve into the art of world-building, where you'll learn to create immersive and captivating settings that enhance your storytelling. Until then, may your suspense be as thrilling as a high-speed chase and you're pacing as mesmerizing as a hypnotic melody!

Chapter 19:
Crafting Immersive Worlds and Vivid Settings

Ahoy, world-builder extraordinaire! In this chapter, we're embarking on a grand adventure through the art of crafting immersive worlds and vivid settings. Picture it as sculpting the very landscapes of your narrative, painting them with detail and color, and inviting your readers to step into these enchanting realms. So, grab your literary paintbrush, and let's dive into the boundless seas of storytelling's world-building wonders!

World-Building: Creating Universes

World-building is the art of creating entire universes within your narrative. Here's how to make your worlds come alive:

◇ **Consistency:** Maintain consistency in your world's rules, cultures, and logic. It's like establishing the laws of physics in your universe.

◇ **Culture and History:** Develop cultures and histories for your worlds. What are their traditions, values, and conflicts? It's like building the rich tapestry of a civilization's past.

◇ **Unique Elements:** Infuse your world with unique elements, whether it's fantastical creatures, advanced technology, or magical systems. It's like adding rare gems to a treasure chest.

Setting Descriptions: Painting with Words

Setting descriptions are like painting vivid landscapes with words. Here's how to bring your settings to life:

◈ **Sensory Details:** Engage readers' senses by describing sights, sounds, smells, tastes, and textures. It's like inviting them to step into the scene.

◈ **Character's Perspective:** Describe settings through your characters' perspectives. How do they feel about their surroundings? It's like seeing the world through their eyes.

◈ **Symbolism:** Use setting symbolism to enhance your narrative. A dark, imposing castle might symbolize tyranny, while a sun-drenched meadow could signify hope.

Weather and Atmosphere: Mood Enhancers

Weather and atmosphere can set the mood for your scenes:

◈ **Weather's Impact:** Weather can affect characters' actions and emotions. A thunderstorm can heighten tension, while a clear, starry night can evoke tranquility.

◈ **Atmosphere's Influence:** Describe the overall atmosphere of a place – is it welcoming or foreboding? It's like setting the tone for a grand performance.

◈ **Symbolic Weather:** Consider using weather symbolically. A sudden rain shower might symbolize cleansing or renewal, while fog can signify mystery and uncertainty.

Incorporating History: Layers of Depth

Incorporating history adds layers of depth to your settings:

◇ **Historical Events:** Develop historical events that have shaped your world. These events can have lasting impacts on characters and societies.

◇ **Ruins and Artifacts:** Include ruins, artifacts, and remnants of the past in your settings. They offer clues to your world's history.

◇ **Legends and Myths:** Legends and myths can enrich your world's lore. Characters may reference these tales or seek to uncover their truths.

Transporting Readers: The Ultimate Goal

The ultimate goal of crafting immersive worlds and vivid settings is to transport readers to new and captivating realms:

◇ **Engagement:** Engage readers' imaginations by offering them a world to explore and become a part of.

◇ **Involvement:** Make readers feel involved in the settings, as if they're walking alongside your characters.

◇ **Emotional Connection:** Create emotional connections between readers and your world, so they care about its fate and characters.

Interactive World-Building

Consider interactive world-building, where readers can explore and engage with your world beyond the narrative:

◇ **Maps and Diagrams:** Include maps and diagrams in your E-book to help readers visualize your world's geography or complex systems.

◈ **Appendices:** Add appendices or glossaries with explanations of key terms, cultures, or historical events.

◈ **Fan Engagement:** Encourage fan engagement by inviting readers to create fan fiction, artwork, or discussions about your world.

The Power of Settings

Settings are more than just backdrops; they're characters in their own right, influencing the story and characters:

◈ **Conflict Catalyst:** Settings can spark conflicts or provide challenges. A treacherous mountain range can be a formidable obstacle.

◈ **Symbolic Significance:** Settings can hold symbolic significance, reflecting characters' internal struggles or the story's themes.

◈ **Mood and Atmosphere:** Settings contribute to the story's mood and atmosphere, affecting how readers perceive events.

Your World-Building Odyssey

With these techniques at your fingertips, your world-building will become an odyssey of creativity and immersion, inviting readers to journey through the worlds you've meticulously crafted.

In the final chapter, we'll explore the art of the unforgettable ending, where you'll learn to leave readers with a lasting impression and a sense of closure. Until then, may your worlds be as vivid as dreams and your settings as enchanting as fairytales!

Chapter 20:
Crafting Unforgettable Endings and Leaving a Lasting Impression

Ahoy, master storyteller! In this final chapter, we're embarking on a grand finale, exploring the art of crafting unforgettable endings that will linger in your readers' hearts and minds. Picture it as the grand finale of a fireworks display, where every burst leaves the audience in awe. So, let's light up the literary sky, and dive into the exhilarating world of storytelling's triumphant conclusions!

Endings: The Culmination of the Journey

Endings are the culmination of the journey, the crescendo of your narrative symphony. Here's how to craft endings that resonate:

◇ **Satisfying Resolution:** Provide a satisfying resolution to the story's central conflict. It's like the final chord of a beautiful melody.

◇ **Character Growth:** Show how characters have evolved and grown throughout the narrative. It's the character's solo performance.

◇ **Themes and Messages:** Revisit the story's themes and messages, reinforcing their significance. It's like the moral of the tale.

Types of Endings: Choosing Your Crescendo

Consider different types of endings to suit your narrative:

◈ **Happy Endings:** Characters achieve their goals, conflicts are resolved, and there's a sense of joy or fulfillment. It's like a jubilant fanfare.

◈ **Tragic Endings:** Characters face defeat or loss, often due to their flaws or circumstances. It's like a haunting, melancholic ballad.

◈ **Open Endings:** Leave some elements unresolved, allowing readers to imagine the future. It's like a cliffhanger that leaves them hanging in suspense.

Emotional Impact: Tugging Heartstrings

Endings should evoke emotions that linger:

◈ **Tug at Heartstrings:** Make readers feel deeply. It's like a poignant melody that brings tears to their eyes.

◈ **Empathy:** Ensure readers empathize with characters' journeys and choices. It's like walking in their shoes.

◈ **Resonance:** Create moments that resonate with readers on a personal level, making them reflect on their own lives.

Character Arcs: Transformation's Echo

Character arcs should find closure, echoing the journey they've undertaken:

◈ **Full Circle:** Characters might return to where they started, but they're not the same. It's like completing a heroic quest.

◈ **Lessons Learned:** Characters should have learned valuable lessons. It's like the wisdom gained from a wise elder.

◈ **Legacy:** Consider the legacy characters leave behind, whether through their actions or impact on others.

Surprises and Twists: A Final Flourish

Endings can contain surprises or twists that leave readers astonished:

◈ **Revelations:** Reveal hidden truths or mysteries that have been simmering throughout the narrative. It's like the final, unexpected plot twist.

◈ **Character Choices:** Characters' choices can be surprising and unexpected, leading to powerful conclusions.

◈ **Subverting Expectations:** Consider subverting genre or storytelling conventions to keep readers guessing.

The Power of Symbolism: A Parting Image

Endings often include powerful symbolic elements:

◈ **Objects:** Symbolic objects can represent characters' journeys or the story's themes. It's like a treasured memento.

◈ **Actions:** Characters' final actions can carry deep symbolic meaning. It's like a profound gesture.

◈ **Metaphors:** Employ metaphors that encapsulate the essence of the story. It's like a riddle waiting to be unraveled.

Reader Reflection: The Ultimate Goal

The ultimate goal of crafting unforgettable endings is to leave readers with a sense of fulfillment and reflection:

⬦ **Closure:** Provide closure to the central narrative while leaving room for readers to ponder its deeper meaning.

⬦ **Lasting Impression:** Craft an ending that lingers in readers' minds long after they've closed the E-book.

⬦ **Emotional Catharsis:** Offer emotional catharsis, allowing readers to process the journey's emotional weight.

The Journey's End and a New Beginning

With these techniques at your disposal, you'll be able to craft endings that are not just conclusions but also new beginnings, sparking readers' imaginations and inviting them to embark on their own storytelling adventures.

And so, our journey through the art of storytelling comes to an end. But remember, every ending is a new beginning, and the world of storytelling is vast and ever-evolving. As you set sail on your own literary voyage, may your stories be as timeless as legends and as boundless as the imagination itself!

Don't miss out!

Visit the website below and you can sign up to receive emails whenever Richard Krause publishes a new book. There's no charge and no obligation.

https://books2read.com/r/B-A-FEUW-INQOC

BOOKS 2 READ

Connecting independent readers to independent writers.

Did you love *EBook Entrepreneur: Crafting Your Path to Profit*? Then you should read *The Writer's Odyssey: Crafting Your Literary Legacy, A New Writer's Guide Book*[1] by Richard Krause!

Embark on an extraordinary journey into the captivating world of writing with *" The Writer's Odyssey: Crafting Your Literary Legacy, A New Writer's Guide Book "*. This enlightening guide takes aspiring authors on a voyage through the art and craft of storytelling, from the inception of a writer's dreams to the thrilling adventure of self-expression.

Discover the power of words as you explore the unique tapestry of your imagination. From the first spark of inspiration to the triumph of completing your manuscript, you'll find inspiration and guidance to fuel your creative journey. Uncover the secrets of compelling

---

1. https://books2read.com/u/4A2MVq

2. https://books2read.com/u/4A2MVq

characters, immersive settings, and gripping plots that will keep readers turning pages.

But this book is more than just a guide to the craft; it's a testament to the resilience and determination that define a true writer. Learn how to overcome writer's block, embrace constructive criticism, and persevere through the highs and lows of your writing adventure.

Join a vibrant writing community, connect with fellow authors, and find the support and encouragement you need to flourish. Cultivate your unique voice, explore diverse genres, and celebrate the joy of creative exploration.

Your writing adventure begins here, and every chapter is a milestone in your literary legacy. Whether you dream of becoming a best-selling author, a poet, or simply desire to share your stories with the world, *"The Writer's Odyssey: Crafting Your Literary Legacy, A New Writer's Guide Book"* will be your steadfast companion.

So, new authors, take that first step and let your journey as a writer commence. The blank pages before you are waiting to be transformed into worlds of your creation. Are you ready to craft your literary legacy? It's time to pick up your pen, open your laptop, and begin your *"The Writer's Odyssey: Crafting Your Literary Legacy"*, today. Your words have the power to inspire, entertain, and leave a lasting legacy. Happy writing!

Read more at https://rkrause45.wixsite.com/mysite.

Also by Richard Krause

The Elderly Trap: Uncovering Scams and Reclaiming Security in the Golden Years.
The Spice Cabinet Apothecary: Natural Health at Your Fingertips"
EBook Entrepreneur: Crafting Your Path to Profit
The Writer's Odyssey: Crafting Your Literary Legacy, A New Writer's Guide Book
From Words To Wealth: Mastering Freelance Writing
The Morning Elixir of Life: The History and Art of Coffee

Watch for more at https://rkrause45.wixsite.com/mysite.

About the Author

Mr. Krause now resides in the Misty Mountains of West Virginia with his lovely wife of 42 years and their three furry four-legged children, Lexi, Aesop, and Kodi. He also has two adult human children. He is 70-plus years of age and has been writing most of his life.

He spent 60 years home-based in Southwestern Florida. During his military career, he saw 22 foreign countries and all fifty of the United States.

He is a retired government worker, with an extensive background in Environmental Protection. He holds a Degree in Network Engineering and Administration specializing in Computer Security, and has a background in both public and private security.

He has been writing professionally now since 1982. For many years he attempted publishing through mainstream publishing but sadly was overlooked. That is when he decided to go the Indie route. In 2018 he published his first book through KDP, it was *"The Book on Evil, Wicked, Mean & Nasty: A Whimsical Guide to Payback and Revenge"* other titles are *"The Fine Art of Getting Even, a Comical Approach to Revenge"*, *"The Ancient Wisdom of an Old Shadow Warrior"*,*"The Plucking of The Golden Years Goose"*, and *"How to Find Your Way in The Internet Jungle, a Guidebook for Work-At-Homers"*.

He has also created and published five low-content journals, *"My Fishing Log Book"*, *"The Traveling Man's Journal"*, *"My Bedside Dream Journal"*, *"My Writing Idea Book"*, *"The Adventurer's*

Notebook" all of which are available on that big box store on the Internet.

Besides reading and writing he is an enthusiastic fisherman, his hobbies are, building and painting 54mm military figures, cutting and polishing semi-precious gemstones, creating unique hand-crafted jewelry, and the restoration of vintage and antique weapons.

He has studied several forms of oriental martial arts for over 50 years. But sadly due to health concerns is no longer able to practice.

Read more at https://rkrause45.wixsite.com/mysite.